Volcano

Jungle

waves

House
Sea views

13°. 15' south

Vegetable
garden

Bumble Bee
crash lands ✕

✕
Sea chest

Lagoon
(safe swimming)

Best fishing
spot

Gap
in
reef

Fruit trees →

← Sun sets

Sun rises →

163°. 05' west

For Aotearoa
(Land of the Long White Cloud)

British Library Cataloguing
in Publication Data
Treloar, Bruce
Bumble's Island.
I. Title
823 [J]   PZ7

ISBN 0-370-30961-8

© Bruce Treloar 1984
Printed and bound in Great Britain for
The Bodley Head Ltd
9 Bow Street, London WC2E 7AL
by William Clowes Ltd, Beccles
First published 1984

BUMBLE'S ISLAND

BRUCE TRELOAR

THE BODLEY HEAD

London · Sydney · Toronto

Mr Bumble sang to his machine as they flew. His beautiful, home-made flying machine, *Bumble Bee*, had flown perfectly but now, leaking fuel and far out above the ocean, Mr Bumble knew that they must come down. Not far ahead was a large white cloud.

"That means land," said Mr Bumble. But as he circled above the island, he could see nowhere at all to put *Bumble Bee* down. Mr Bumble prepared to ditch his machine into the lagoon.

"Not too much damage, I hope," Mr Bumble mumbled to himself.

Struggling, he heaved the broken *Bumble Bee* out of the shallow water. Then he ate his last sandwich, drained his tea flask and set off to explore.

It looked a perfect island.

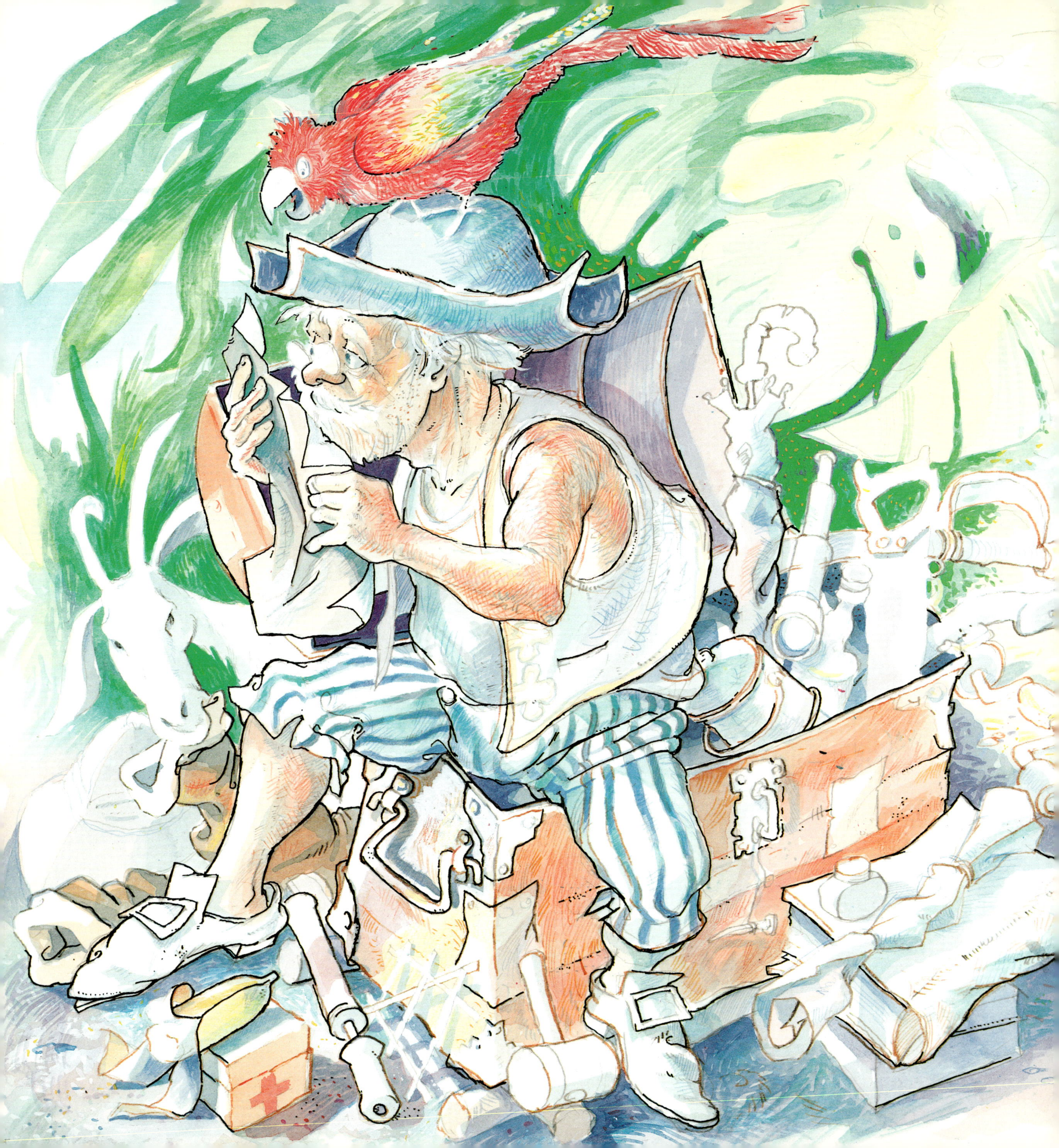

Amongst the trees Mr Bumble found an old wooden sea chest. A goat sat beside it. A parrot sat on the lid.

"Ben Gunn, Ben Gunn," repeated the parrot over and over again.

Inside the chest, brimful with useful things, was a note:

Dear Traveller, Use what you will. Leave what you can. Best wishes. A Seafarer.

"Very thoughtful," said Mr Bumble, and he set about building a house.

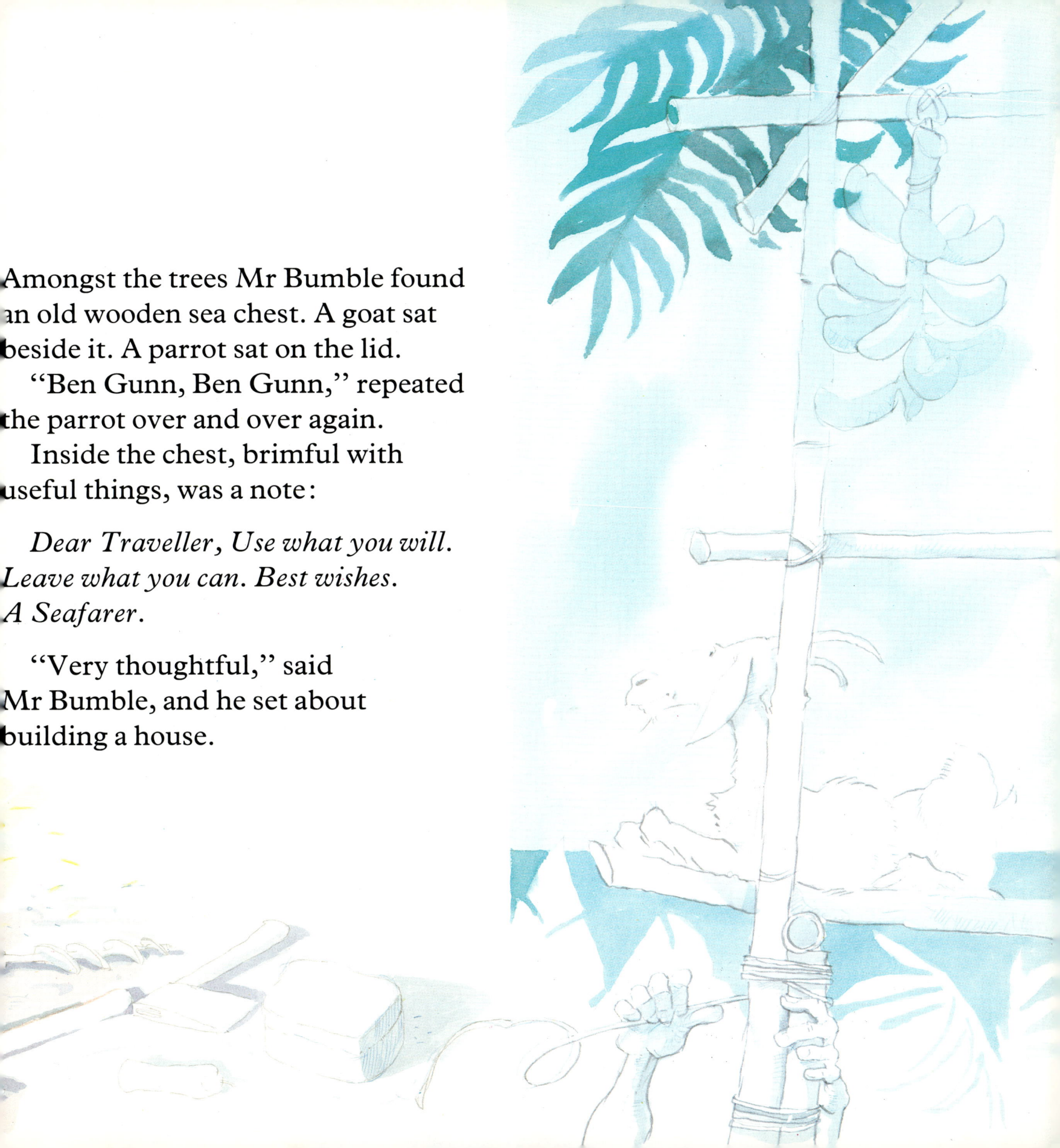

Mr Bumble was very content. Each evening he sat with his companions, Billy and Ben Gunn, and wrote up the ship's log he had found in the sea chest. He noted their position (which didn't change), the number of days (which did), and the weather (which didn't much).

Position 13°15' south x 163°05' west
Day   : 90
Weather: Rain, hot, south-east wind

Sprayed vegetables (used bike pump)
planted corn, pumpkin seed
Fish for dinner
Trim Billy's toe nails

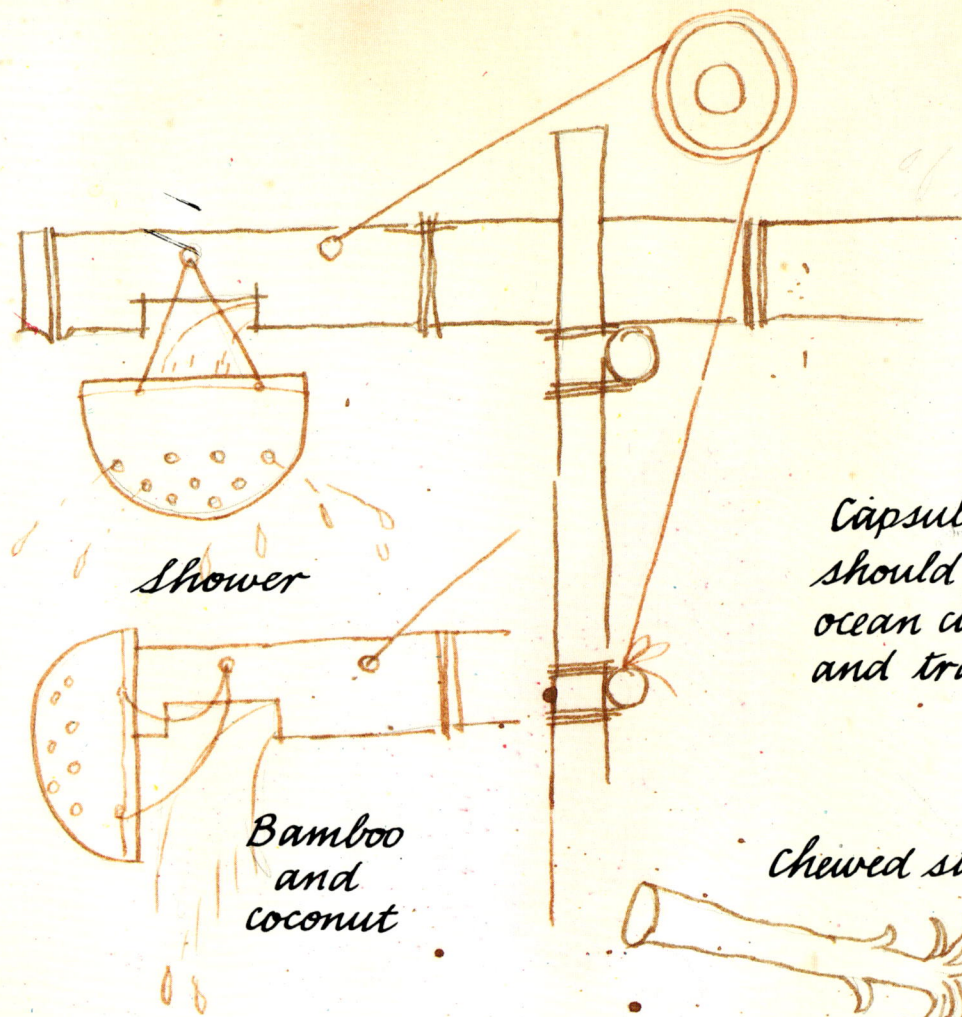

Water-
proof
capsu
to sen
note
home

Ballast

Shower

Bamboo
and
coconut

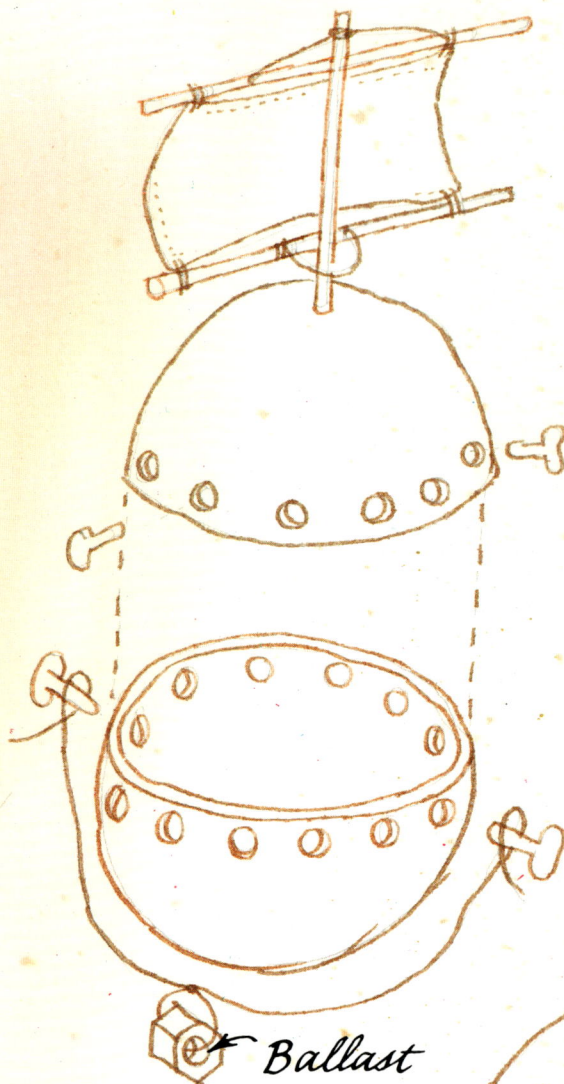

Capsule
should follow
ocean current
and trade winds

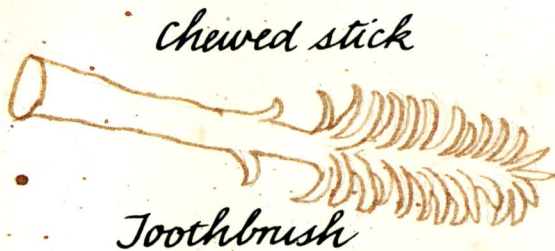

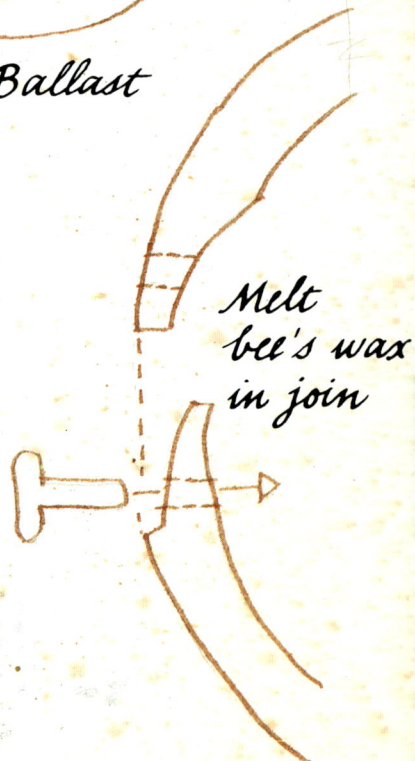

Melt
bee's wax
in join

Chewed stick

Toothbrush

On cool nights Mr Bumble played his fiddle or his flute and danced in the moonlight with the goat – who wasn't very good at dancing.

Mr Bumble was enjoying his adventure, although he did sometimes miss his junk yard back home and his good friends, Timothy and Emily the hen.

One night, when Mr Bumble was sitting mending his trousers, there came a long, low, rumbling sound. The whole house shook. The table shuddered and the shadows trembled.

"Volcano!" whispered Mr Bumble.

"Abandon ship! Abandon ship!" screeched Ben Gunn.

Mr Bumble knew that they must leave the island. But how? *Bumble Bee* would never fly again.

All that night Mr Bumble sat thinking and calculating, scribbling plans and diagrams.

The volcano heaved and moaned.

The sun rose.

"Solved it!" cried Mr Bumble at last. "I've got it!—

"But can I build it?"

Position : 13° 15' south x 163° 05' west

Day : 305

Weather : Mild, fine - seas calm   Set capsule afloat

Plans for G.V. Bumble Bee (Gliding Vessel)

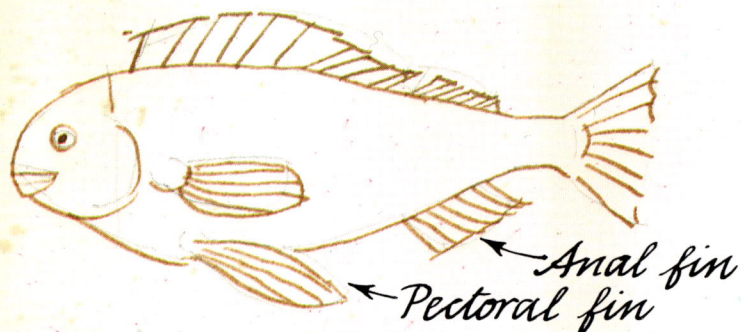

common fish

Pectoral fin

Anal fin

Flying fish
enlarged pectoral fin

steerage

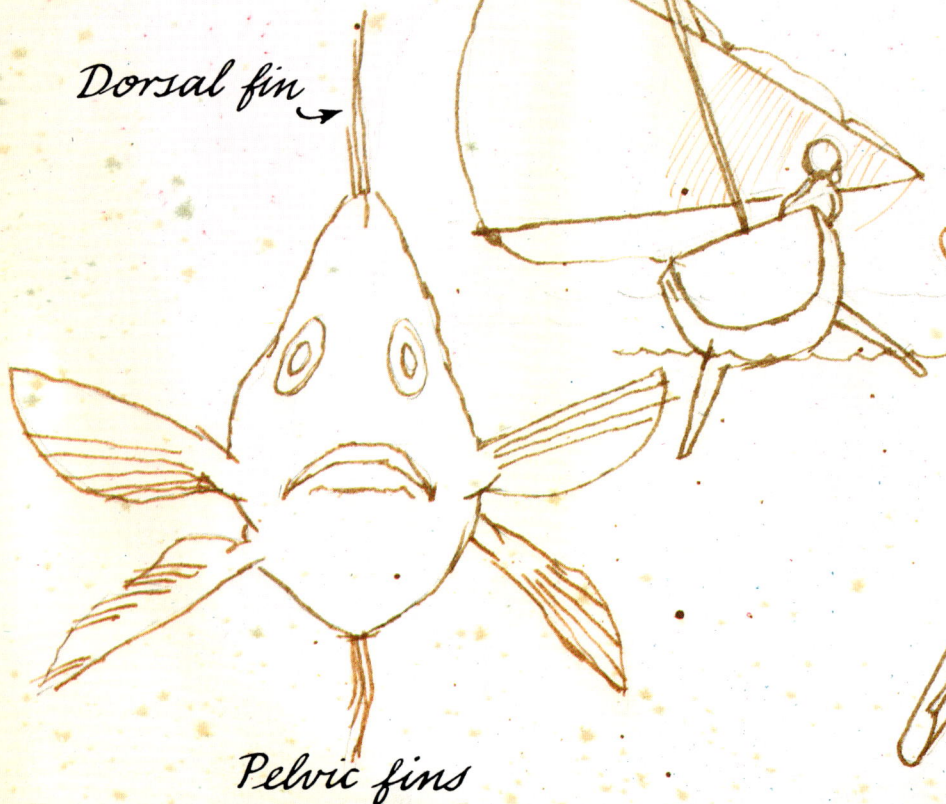

Dorsal fin

Pelvic fins

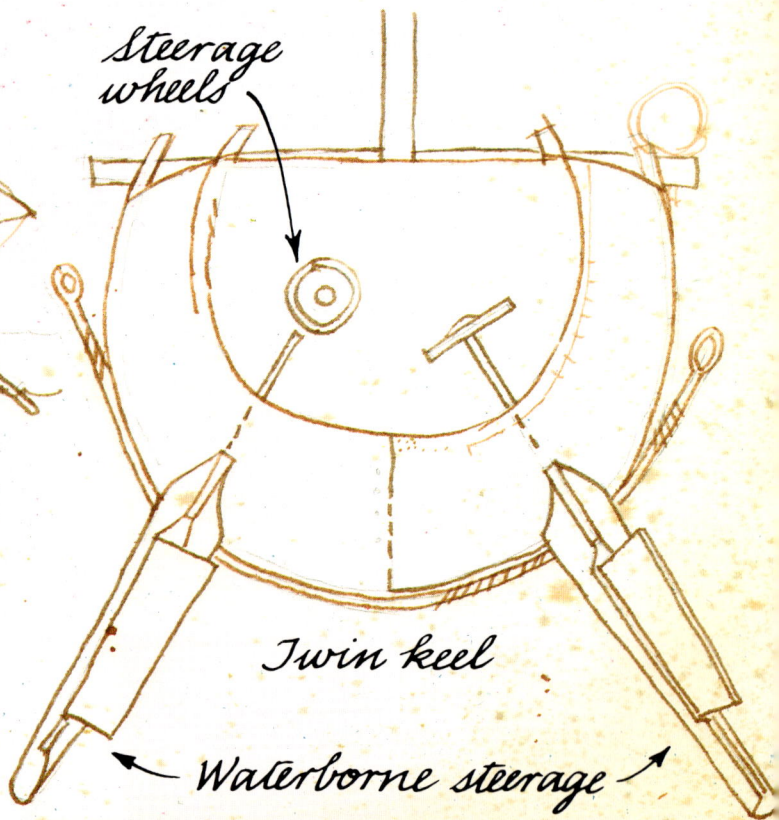

Steerage
wheels

Twin keel

Waterborne steerage

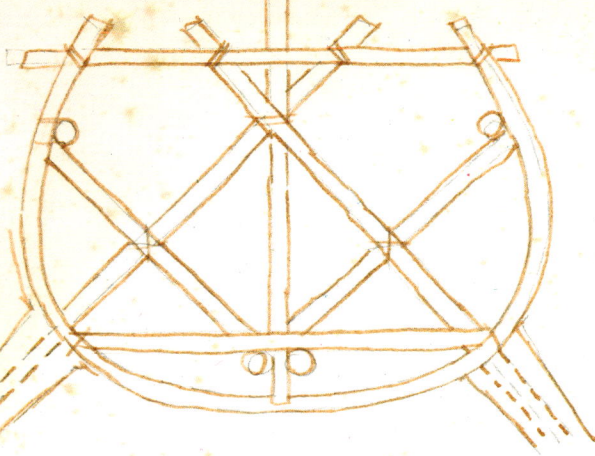

Middle
cross section

Back end

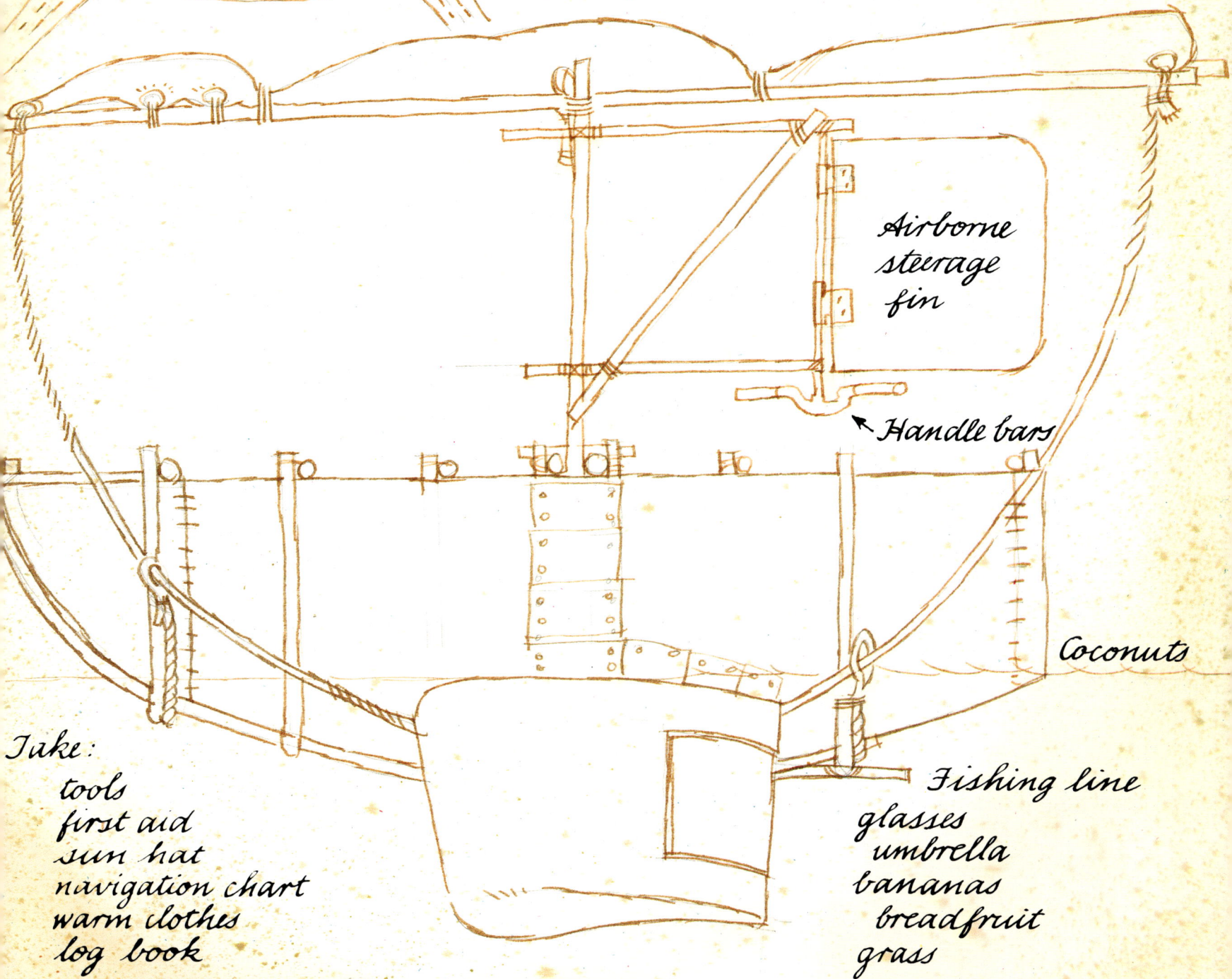

Airborne
steerage
fin

← Handle bars

Coconuts

Take:
  tools
  first aid
  sun hat
  navigation chart
  warm clothes
  log book

Fishing line
  glasses
  umbrella
  bananas
  breadfruit
  grass

Although Mr Bumble was exhausted, he wasted no time in starting work on *G.V. Bumble Bee*. Piece by piece the old flying machine was transformed into an ocean-going Bumble boat.

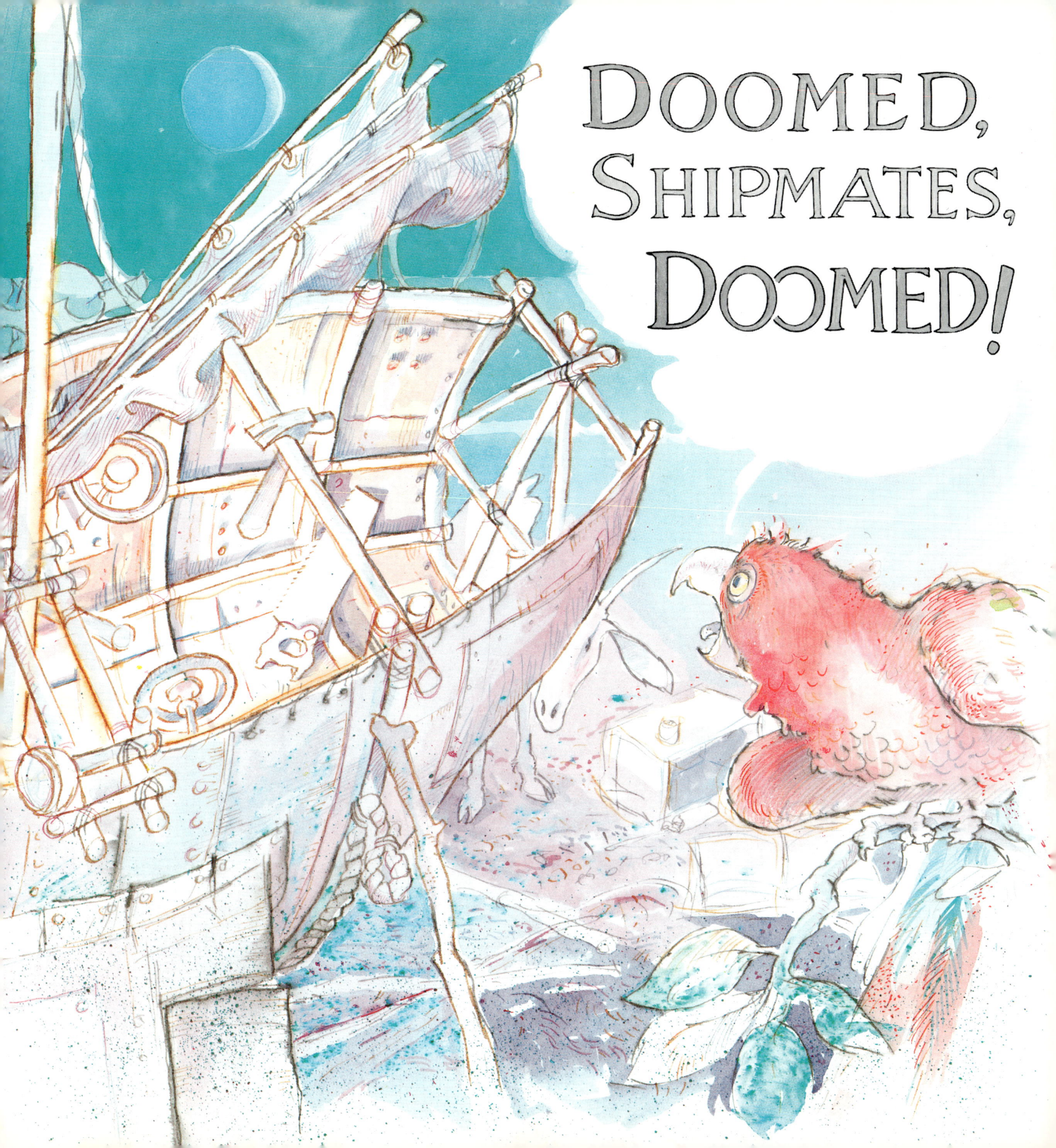

DOOMED,
SHIPMATES,
DOOMED!

Mr Bumble repacked the sea chest, signed the note simply "B", and closed the lid. He loaded his companions into *G.V. Bumble Bee*, heaved it into the lagoon and set the sail. A strong wind spread the canvas and carried them out into the ocean.

They took a last look at the island.
Smoke and ash flew into the air and
the mountain roared. The volcano
had erupted.

Mr Bumble steered a course
homeward, following the moon and
the stars.

Sailing, gliding. Sailing and
gliding.

Each day he kept notes in the old
ship's log.

Position : 29°.05' *south* x 167°.59' *east*
Day : 366 Thursday, October
Weather : Wonderful (Spring)

"A grand adventure that was, Tim," said Mr Bumble. "But it's great to be back home."

"What shall we do next, Mr B?" asked Tim.

"Well," said Mr Bumble, "what about another cup o' tea?"

163°. 05 west